Chris Hegarty is a barrister practising in London specialising in professional negligence litigation with a particular focus on financial services claims for individuals.

A Practical Guide to Financial Services Claims

A Practical Guide to Financial Services Claims

Chris Hegarty, M.Eng,
Barrister

Law Brief Publishing

Published 2018 by Law Brief Publishing, an imprint of Law Brief Publishing Ltd
30 The Parks
Minehead
Somerset
TA24 8BT

www.lawbriefpublishing.com

Paperback: 978-1-911035-55-8

To Sarah, Jo and Madeleine

PREFACE

Financial services claims arise out of a variety of financial products and services which have been provided in unsuitable or inappropriate ways and ultimately caused significant loss to the customer. The development of more innovative financial products and the gradual opening of access to these to increasingly smaller businesses and, eventually, individuals has led to the recent expansion in litigation.

The purpose of this text is not to deliver a work on financial professionals, services, products and regulation – there are numerous texts addressing these numerous issues and I heartily recommend further reading in those directions which are appropriate to your own interests and practice. These subjects however would require a tome of numerous volumes rather than this brief practical guide.

My aim is to discuss the specific intersection of the laws of tort and contract with financial services and where this gives rise to claims against financial institutions and professionals. I do not assume more than a practical knowledge of tort and contract law and endeavour to assume no pre-existing knowledge of financial services law and regulation.

I trust you find this helpful as a reference and introductory text.

The law is stated as at 25 March 2018, however references to the COB rules in the FSA Handbook which are no longer in force are to that version which was last in force (31 October 2007). Notably, due to the incremental changes in the FCA Handbook no excerpts are quoted as it is unwise to rely upon a version fixed in time, instead the reader should consider the version in force as at the time of the problem under consideration.

Chris Hegarty
Barrister
July 2018

P.S. Following submission of this manuscript the decision has been handed down in Parmar v Barclays Bank [2018] EWHC 1027 (Ch) and there are potential implications for interest rate hedging product cases, and potentially more broadly.

CONTENTS

CHAPTER ONE
INTRODUCTION: A BRIEF HISTORY OF FINANCIAL SERVICES

Before 2001

Financial services regulation had an epoch defining moment in 2000 when the Financial Services and Markets Act 2000 ("FSMA") was passed. This swept away the previous regime of self-regulation of the industry by the various Self Regulatory Organisations ("SROs"), replacing it with regulation by the Financial Services Authority.

I do not propose to dwell on the previous regime because as at 2017 almost all of those cases arising under the SRO regime have passed and such a discussion is of purely historic interest; save only where the application of section 32 Limitation Act 1980 enables such a claim to be brought.

The dawn of a new day

On 1 December 2001 the *Financial Services and Markets Act 2000* and its legion of supporting instruments came into force.

A new, singular Handbook was designated as the rulebook for all financial services businesses and was broken down into various parts and sections all of which clearly specified to whom and in what circumstances they applied.

This was, in the UK, the first major example of outcomes focused regulation where the regulatory objectives would be set, a specific business however could comply in any fashion it wished, although the business itself bore the risk of failures in effective compliance. To this end a set of overarching Principles were set down at the start of the Handbook.

Atop the ordinary contractual and tortious causes of action a specific statutory cause of action was created for breach of the rules set out in the Handbook (where permitted) in section 150 of FSMA, specifically intended to grant to individuals[1] the ability to sue for breaches of the Handbook and therefore provide a simpler and more direct remedy than an action in negligence.

The most important rulebooks when considering claims by a customer against a financial services business are the various Conduct of Business rulebooks. These set out the rules applicable to a business when undertaking business either generally (COB) or in relation to insurance (ICOB) or mortgages (MCOB). These rules were developed as a successor to the rules of the various SROs with the advantage of additional oversight and the opportunity to correct any perceived shortcomings or failings and so were intended to provide a clear set of standards to which financial services providers could expect to be held.

COB introduced concepts, particularly *suitability,* which form the cornerstone for the majority of financial services claims. This idea of suitability, and a framework for the issues to be factored into the assessment of suitability, was a major shift in the delivery of financial services and opened up a much more structured approach to the delivery of effective financial advice, sale of financial products and the proper consideration of whether such advice and sale was performed effectively and in a fashion which ensured that the consumer was properly protected, informed and advised.

---

1 See the Rights of Action Regulations

Europe strikes back

Whilst the developments in the UK with FSMA continued, the Europe-wide regulation and oversight of cross-border financial services did not stand still. In numerous areas EU regulations imposed requirements and standards to establish a solid basis for a common market in financial services.

From a consumer perspective the single most significant instrument to emanate from Europe was the Markets in Financial Instruments Directive[2] ("MiFID"). As a Directive this necessitated new rules replacing certain significant parts of the FSA Handbook – particularly those relating to conduct of business. Therefore, with effect from 1 November 2007, the Conduct of Business Sourcebook ("COBS") replaced COB.

Fortunately for practical purposes the changes involved are not enormous, MiFID and therefore COBS, set out rules for the conduct of business which were significantly influenced by COB. The concept of suitability was therefore retained albeit rephrased and the additional concept of *appropriateness* introduced.

Appropriateness, in this specific context, is set out in COBS 10 to increase the standard of care applying to less mainstream products where suitability does not otherwise apply.

Return of The Bank of England

Following the financial crises of the late 2000s a major reorganisation of financial services was undertaken, resulting in the Financial Services Act 2012 (the "*2012 Act*"). The single greatest

2 Directive 2004/39/EC

change was the separation of responsibility of regulation of large financial institutions from the FSA – which was renamed the Financial Conduct Authority ("*FCA*") in the process – to the Bank of England (although under its title of the Prudential Regulation Authority, "*PRA*", for these purposes).

One slight but noteworthy change at this time for the purposes of claims against financial professionals was the relocation of the Section 150 FSMA cause of action to section 138D FSMA.

And next?

On the horizon we have MiFID II[3], which is expected to bring into scope newer and more novel investments and provide enhanced protections. With commencement dates over the coming years, it remains to be seen how litigation involving financial products will evolve in response to the actions of financial services firms in providing their services.

3 Directive 2014/65/EU

CHAPTER TWO LEGAL BASIS FOR FINANCIAL SERVICES CLAIMS

It may be trite to state that in order to formulate a claim it is necessary to identify:

1. the parties;
2. the legal causes of action;
3. the facts giving rise to those causes of action;
4. the loss occurring as a result; and
5. the potential defences.

However, in the context of financial services there is a regulatory dimension overlaid upon existing legal and equitable principles. The applicable duties and/or protections imposed by that regulatory dimension are predicated upon the parties and their own particular positions.

For the purposes of clarity, and to align with phrasing used by the FCA, the term "client" refers to the client of the financial services firm, and "firm" refers to the financial services business of any size or form. It should be noted that this means that the "client" also tends to be the claimant in any action and the "firm" the defendant; however this is not necessarily the case.

To consider the legal background to financial services regulation it is necessary to look at one of the key operative parts of FSMA – Part II – which establishes a regulatory perimeter delineating regulated acts from other, unregulated acts, and the prohibitions and penalties for crossing that perimeter without permission. Part II defines the general prohibition (s.19) and a prohibition on financial promotions (s.21), empowers the Treasury to define regulated acts (ss.22 – 22B) and establishes criminal offences (ss.23 – 25). Finally it sets out hard edged provisions as to unenforceability and compensation when regulated acts are done without permission (s.26) or arising out of a prior breach (s.27).

Parties

Claimants

Private persons

In broad terms there are two issues which must be identified for any claimant, are they individual or corporate; and what client categorisation do they fall within.

A significant volume of financial services claims are brought by individuals or businesses who have been misadvised in relation to individual investment products, whole portfolios or pensions.

The right of action under section 150/138D FSMA is restricted to private persons by regulation 6 of the The Financial Services and Markets Act 2000 (Rights of Action) Regulations 2001 (the "*Rights of Action Regulations*"). A private person is defined in regulation 3:

> *"3. (1) In these Regulations, "private person" means—*
>
> *(a) any individual, unless he suffers the loss in question in the course of carrying on—*

(i) any regulated activity; or

(ii) any activity which would be a regulated activity apart from any exclusion made by article 72 of the Regulated Activities Order (overseas persons); and

(b) any person who is not an individual, unless he suffers the loss in question in the course of carrying on business of any kind;

but does not include a government, a local authority (in the United Kingdom or elsewhere) or an international organisation.

(2) For the purposes of paragraph (1)(a), an individual who suffers loss in the course of effecting or carrying out contracts of insurance (within the meaning of article 10 of the Regulated Activities Order) written at Lloyd's is not to be taken to suffer loss in the course of carrying on a regulated activity."

As such natural persons are within the scope of this definition, even if they are engaged in business on their own account. However where the loss falls on a corporate person the second subsection must be considered.

The key issue is whether the loss is sustained "in the course of carrying on business". The issue was considered fully in Titan Steel Wheels v RBS[1] and Camerata v Credit Suisse[2]; and interpreted very broadly so that almost any commercial undertaking (other than natural persons) with a view to a profit would be found to be excluded from the definition of a "private person". Permission was

1 [2010] EWHC 211 (Comm)

2 [2012] EWHC 7 (Comm)

granted in MTR Bailey v Barclays[3] to appeal on this issue – however no substantive appeal was ever heard therefore there is no appellate authority.

Non-private persons

Any person not being a private person does not attract those statutory causes of actions in accordance with the Rights of Action Regulations and so is only able to rely upon contractual, tortious and fiduciary duties.

Client categorisation

Whether a private person or not any client of a financial services business must, per COBS 3.3.1 R (formerly COB 4.1.4 R) of the Handbook, must be categorised:

1. Private Customer (COB) / Retail Client (COBS);
2. Intermediate Client (COB) / Professional Client (COBS); or
3. Market Counterparty (COB) / Eligible Counterparty (COBS).

These categories within COB and COBS are equivalents which are only re-phrasings of the same group. Notably, a client who would be a particular category objectively can be categorised upwards or downwards by agreement between the firm and the client in certain circumstances.

3 [2015] EWCA Civ 667

Private Customers / Retail clients

These achieve the highest level of protection as they are not financial professionals. Provided that a notation exists in the Handbook confirming that a relevant Handbook rule is actionable it is open to such a client to rely upon it.

Typically most individuals will be private customers or retail clients unless another category applies to them.

Intermediate/professionals

This categorisation applies to financial firms and other larger businesses. These are, often, professionals who work in the financial sector such as stockbrokers, financial advisers and bankers; this category also includes larger non-financial businesses (COBS 3.5.2 R). Such people may be 'downgraded' to private/retail clients by agreement and therefore attract all of the protections applicable to private/retail clients.

Notably, businesses may be required by a financial services firm to be categorised as intermediate/professional clients in order that they can deal with the firm. This still necessitates the business meeting the requirements in COBS 3.5.3 R regarding elective classification.

When dealing with such clients in this category it is important to note carefully whether each rule sought to be applied is applicable to such clients. COB and COBS both include in their application provisions clear delineation of those rules which are varied or disapplied in relation to such clients.

Where the regulatory provisions are retained the guidance herein may be applied to such cases. However, the legal principles not reliant upon the Handbook may be relied upon where one party is an intermediate/professional client; issues of bargaining power may however be brought into play in such cases.

COBS 3.5.9 R provides that such clients could be required to be re-classified as retail clients if they no longer meet the requirements of their existing classification.

Market counterparties

Market or Eligible Counterparties are exactly what they sound like – and as such attract the lowest level of protection. Claims involving such entities have more in common with high value commercial litigation and with both parties subject to regulation are beyond the scope of this book.

As with intermediate/professional clients the Handbook rules applicable when dealing with such a client are reduced.

Sophisticated and High-Net Worth Individuals

These are not a separate classification, however, the concept is better addressed in this stage than (as it strictly is) as a defence to certain allegations of breach of duty.

There are restrictions on promotion of collective investment schemes to ordinary retail investors. However by statutory instrument and Handbook rule (COB 3 Annex 5 R/ COBS 4.12 R) specific circumstances have been set out which, if complied with, allow such promotions to be made to individuals.

The certification options can be found in the Financial Services and Markets Act 2000 (Promotion of Collective Investment

Schemes) Regulations 2001 (the "PCIS Order")[4]. These requirements were rephrased significantly in 2005[5]. The formalities remained but the form of certificates were significantly revised.

These are however purely a gateway into enabling promotion of such schemes – therefore before raising such schemes the certification process needs to be completed. Merely adding such forms as 'paperwork' after the fact is likely to remain a strict breach of the prohibition on such financial promotions.

The alternative in COB/COBS schedules a set of circumstances in which the firm may rely upon alternatives to enable such promotions.

Defendants

Regulated Financial Advisers

Most financial services claims involve an 'adviser' of some sort. Strictly, a financial adviser must be authorised individually and working for an authorised business. Since 1 January 2013 (the commencement into force of the Retail Distribution Review or "RDR") the adviser must also hold qualifications meeting level 4 on the European Qualifications Framework; and in any event qualification set out in TC Appendix 4.1 of the Handbook.

Once qualified and working for a firm which holds the relevant permissions, which has to explicitly permit the firm to, inter alia,

---

4 SI 2000/1060

5 The Financial Services and Markets Act 2000 (Financial Promotion and Promotion of Collective Investment Schemes) (Miscellaneous Amendments) Order 2005, SI 2005/270

advise on and arrange various sorts of regulated product; the individual adviser must be noted as holding Controlled Function "CF30 Customer".

The FCA operates a register of all authorised financial professionals which can be located at https://register.fca.org.uk/ and individuals along with the relevant business can be located, along with confirmation that they were authorised at the relevant time and the scope of the firm's current authorisations.

Financial advisers themselves however come in two distinct groups – the truly 'independent' financial adviser who is required to advise on products across the whole of the market; and the 'restricted' financial adviser who is tied to a particular provider's products, often their employer's or network's range.

The distinction can only be clearly seen when the adviser issues a Key Facts and Initial Disclosure Document which set out key information regarding the adviser, their services and the cost of this.

If a regulated person acts outwith their authorisation this is not a breach of the general prohibition and does not attract criminal sanction per section 20 FSMA.

Banks and other restricted financial advisers

In the same fashion as other regulated financial advisers larger institutions have employed or otherwise tied advisers. These are identifiable in that they are often not able to advise on the whole of the market and instead only their own range of products.

Typically, a high street bank, for example, if offering financial products necessitating advice will be able to provide the necessary advice.

Other important examples include IFA networks where the principal permits the financial advisers only to advise on a restricted range of products may need to be treated as restricted advisers, although some networks may have an approval process to enable their advisers to deal with other products and so may be considered whole of market. The Key Facts documents issued will clearly state what variety of adviser is being dealt with.

Appointed Representatives and their Principals

There are two types of person who are able to undertake regulated financial services work without being in breach of the general prohibition. The clearest are those who are authorised pursuant to Part 4A (previously Part IV) of FSMA ("Authorised Persons").

An alternative to obtaining such full authorisation for financial professionals is to enter into an appointed representative agreement with an authorised person (holding the necessary permissions for the work being undertaken) under section 39 of FSMA. Such an agreement must be in writing and set out the scope of the work that the authorised principal accepts responsibility for.

Such appointed representatives will often pay fees (or otherwise cause remuneration to flow) to their principal and in return for which will be able to offer services without carrying their own overheads of compliance and insurance services.

However, if such an appointed representative fails in their duties then the principal is liable:

> *"The principal of an appointed representative is responsible, to the same extent as if he had expressly permitted it, for anything done or omitted by the representative in carrying on the business for which he has accepted responsibility."*[6]

This distinction between the principal's liability and that of the appointed representative is important and it is vital to identify such arrangements early so as to avoid taking steps which are ultimately likely to be ineffective. In particular when looking at dissolved and/or insolvent appointed representatives it may be that there is a principal behind them which can make the ordinary steps of restoration moot.

However, as a pragmatic matter, the liability of the appointed representative itself is not extinguished by section 39 FSMA, therefore where that appointed representative is a viable defendant then it may be possible to look for redress directly. However, the statutory causes of action would not apply to an exempt rather than authorised person and a careful analysis of the merits of taking such steps should always be taken. As the principal is required to meet the appointed representative's liabilities any insurance is likely to be held by the principal.

Other Exempt persons

As with appointed representatives certain professionals (solicitors for example) have, by virtue of the relevant regulator having issued them with rights to practice, an exemption under Part XX FSMA from the requirement to be authorised to provide certain financial

---

6 section 39(3) FSMA

services which would otherwise amount to a breach of the general prohibition.

This exemption is only open to a professional when the strict requirements of s.327 FSMA are met. Individual orders made under s.326 FSMA to designate a professional body are necessary to afford the exemption to those professionals who are authorised by a Relevant Professional Body to be exempted from the general prohibition and to what extent. Such relevant additional order and consequent professional rules must be considered is such a case.

Therefore, by way of example, whilst a solicitor advising on and arranging a policy of after the event insurance is certainly ancillary to the proceedings to which the after the event insurance is being taken out for; a solicitor could not (and should not!) advise on or arrange the obtaining of a life insurance policy even when undertaking other business for that client as such work would be hard to consider ancillary. There may be some blurring of the lines – for example in a property purchase the obtaining of buildings insurance may seem ancillary but it would be incautious for a solicitor to arrange this as it would not be wholly part of the transaction as it continues beyond the purchase. By way of counter example, when acting as a personal representative of an estate it would be an unwise solicitor who failed as a trustee to ensure that property within the estate remained insured.

It is therefore clear that there is a factual inquiry to be undertaken to consider whether a professional is within the scope of their Part XX exemption or not. This is a necessary inquiry as an exempt person, unlike an authorised person, who undertakes financial services work which they are not authorised to do does not have the benefit of the exclusion of criminal liability.

Practically, this means that such an exempt person would be sued in the context of the service they are predominantly providing and a claim relating to issues with such financial services would be brought within a broader negligence claim for the primary service.

Unregulated introducers/advisers

There are a number of related service providers, often branding themselves as 'introducers' who purport to sell or purely introduce customers to financial products.

A pure introducer has a specific exemption in regulation 33 of the RAO which excludes from the activity of "arranging" (notably regulation 25(2) only) steps which are purely providing an introduction of a customer to a financial services business in order for the customer to obtain advice (or, strictly, the exercise of discretion). This is however a very narrow exemption – any step into advising is not exempted.

Unregulated introducers are not required to carry any professional indemnity coverage, nor are they covered by the protection arrangements of the FSCS

Unregulated provision of financial services (as defined in the RAO) directly by an unregulated person gives rise under s.26 FSMA to transactions which may be set aside and compensation paid. The case of Re Whiteley Insurance Consultants[7] considered the issue where an insurance broker did not actually place insurance but instead acted as an insurer itself, and paid out on those claims where there was no underwriter – as such was held to be carrying out the regulated activities of effecting and carrying on insurance business. The other interesting aspect was that as

7 [2008] EWHC 1782 (Ch)

insurance broking was not a regulated activity, Whiteley was not authorised for the entire period and so s.26 was engaged; however from 14 January 2005 when acting as an insurance intermediary was regulated and Whiteley was so authorised, s.26 was no longer available, but s.20 provided a different cause of action for acting outside authorisation.

Such unregulated persons can also, if they find themselves undertaking regulated business in breach of the general prohibition (s.19 FSMA) or the prohibition on financial promotions (s.21 FSMA), find themeselves criminally liable. This is however a criminal issue and one which is outwith the scope of civil claims. Nevertheless, it should be borne in mind in the event that a witness may inadvertently waive their privilege against self-incrimination and a practitioner should be careful to ensure that they do not breach professional rules in such lines of questioning.

Financial product providers

In circumstances where a regulated firm (such as insurer / SIPP / lender) has provided a financial service to a consumer as a result of the actions of an unregulated party acting in breach of the general prohibition there is a specific cause of action in section 27 FSMA:

> *"27 Agreements made through unauthorised persons.*
>
> *(1) An agreement made by an authorised person ("the provider")—*
>
> *(a) in the course of carrying on a regulated activity (not in contravention of the general prohibition), but*
>
> *(b) in consequence of something said or done by another person ("the third party") in the course of a regulated activity carried*

on by the third party in contravention of the general prohibition,

is unenforceable against the other party.

(2) The other party is entitled to recover—

(a) any money or other property paid or transferred by him under the agreement; and

(b) compensation for any loss sustained by him as a result of having parted with it.

(3) "Agreement" means an agreement—

(a) made after this section comes into force; and

(b) the making or performance of which constitutes, or is part of, the regulated activity in question carried on by the provider.

(4) This section does not apply if the regulated activity is accepting deposits."

There is a statutory defence to section 26 and section 27 claims in section 28 FSMA which allows the court to waive the duties imposed where it is just and equitable to do so. It should be noted that this is a somewhat discretionary defence and, practically, likely to be highly fact specific. This has been tested in the context of a regulated mortgage contract in the case of Helden v Strathmore Ltd[8]; in which a regulated mortgage contract came about as a result of an oversight by a conveyancer. The borrower sought to render the charge unenforceable and (save in one respect which related to an unusual loan) was unsuccessful. The Judge's

8 [2011] EWCA Civ 542

decision was upheld in the Court of Appeal on the factual bases in that case, particularly that the lender did not engage in such activity ordinarily, nor other FSMA activities; and, also the general issues relating to the availability of the loans, the use of the money and benefit of it, and the absence of inequality of arms. Such a determination is clearly fact specific but indicates the breadth of discretion in the defence.

Causes of action

Contract

The relationship between the provider of financial services and their client almost always involves a contractual relationship. Locating this requires consideration of the terms of business document along with documents (often titled Key Facts, Information and Disclosure Document (IDD) or Combined Information and Disclosure Document (CIDD)) which contains standardized information disclosures about the service provided – and crucially the terms upon which the provider is to be paid.

It is necessary to identify the scope and extent of the contractual duty accepted so as to ascertain what additional or alternative causes of action or defences may be available.

Basis clauses

The concept of basis clauses has been employed for quite some time in order to set out what is averred to be the basis upon which the parties enter into a contract for the provision of financial services.

These predominantly derive from the concept of contractual estoppel in Springwell v JP Morgan Chase[9] (at pp.179-182) where clauses which genuinely set out the basis upon which the parties intended to contract were upheld, however, where the effect of such clauses is to:

> *"retrospectively to alter the character and effect of what has gone on before and so is in substance an attempt to exclude or restrict liability."*

This apparently simple premise gives rise to factual concerns regarding whether unfair contractual terms and contracting out are engaged if such clauses seek to alter what has gone before. There is some discussion as to whether attempts to rewrite history fall outwith this concept however where no such attempt is made, such clauses appear permissible.

For a detailed discussion see pp.114-117 of Crestsign v National Westminster[10] which clearly balances the issues and, accepting that Crestsign were not a large commercial party, it was found that the basis clauses were properly and sufficiently conveyed to Crestsign and understood as to be effective; in a more consumer context then such clauses may not be as effective. Caution needs to be applied where dealing with less sophisticated clients, or seeking to part company with history as such clauses may not be upheld.

In addition the ordinary limitations in s.3 of the Unfair Contract Terms Act 1977 (now s.62 Consumer Rights Act 2015 for consumer contracts) are applicable unless an apparent exclusion satisfies the requirements of a basis clause. Further, COBS 2.1.2 R (and COB 2.5.3 – 2.5.4 R) prohibit excluding liability under the

---

9 [2010] EWCA Civ 1211

10 [2014] EWHC 3043 (Ch)

regulatory system. Where such an attempt to exclude liability is made regulation 6 of the Rights of Action Regulations extends the section 150/138D FSMA cause of action to other persons. This approach however was unsuccessful in Titan Steel Wheels v RBS[11].

Reported cases considering the issues surrounding exclusions of liability relate to businesses dealing with financial services firms there are no cases regarding private persons or individuals. Thus the interaction with the COBS non exclusion duty and the alternative route to an action under the Rights of Action regulations for an unlawful exclusion remains untested.

The recent decision of the Privy Council in Chen v Ng[12] suggests that the concept of a contractual estoppel is not as firm as the view which was expressed in Springwell v JP Morgan Chase[13]. However, this point has yet to be considered by an English court.

Pre-contractual advice

A not uncommon situation involves the situation where no contract is entered into between a client and financial services firm until the advice is actually being implemented. Without a contract in existence when, for example, information is gathered or a suitability letter is prepared, there can be no breach of a contract.

This was specifically considered in *Worthing v Lloyds*[14], and three possibilities were explored:

---

11 [2010] EWHC 211 (Comm)

12 [2017] UKPC 27 at pp.27 – 38

13 (ibid.)

14 [2015] EWHC 2836 (QBD)

> *"68. There are at least three different ways in which it might be open to the claimants to contend that the defendant was under continuing contractual obligations in respect of the initial investment advice.*
>
> *1) The original investment advice was given under a contract, but the advice, being incorrectly given, did not discharge the defendant's duty under the contract and the defendant remained contractually bound to perform that duty; such performance required the defendant to correct its original advice.*
>
> *2) After the initial investment advice was given, a new contract came into existence, under which the defendant was under an absolute obligation to correct any incorrect advice it had originally given.*
>
> *3) Whether under the contract pursuant to which the initial investment advice was given or under a new contract that came into existence thereafter, the defendant was required to conduct periodic reviews; and in conducting those reviews the defendant was required to exercise reasonable care and skill and to comply with the COBS Rules."*

The first two were disposed of as no contract coming into existence under them; however, the court accepted that, in relation to the ongoing advice, a contract did exist to review with reasonable skill and care.

As such pre-contractual advice and investigations must be carefully plead so as to ensure that the basis is clear to avoid the risk of pleadings which are defective by reason of pleading a simple breach of contract when none subsisted at the time of a relevant breach.

Explicit duties

The contracts proffered by financial services firms vary widely in their length, scope and terms. When contemplating any claim it is vital to ascertain what exactly has been agreed between the client and business, particularly insofar as restrictions on what will be performed.

Identifying the scope of any ongoing advisory duties and the proper construction and application of these is necessary to frame any claim or defence arising out of such a duty. Reasonableness and other phrases which are not quantifiable can lead to significant disputes over what each party meant or understood to be the case.

Implied duties

Whether an explicit duty exists or not it is still possible to rely upon the implied duty in section 13 of the Supply of Goods and Services Act 1982; in cases involving consumers this duty has been relocated to s.49 of the Consumer Rights Act 2015.

That implied duty is to "carry out the service with reasonable care and skill" and is therefore quite broad and requires careful particularisation of the steps said to be necessary to comply.

Tort

There are a variety of tortious causes of action which are available to a claimant, predominantly arising out of the concept of professional negligence. However, despite the modern popularity of the law of negligence and the modelling of many non-contractual obligations in its terms, it is also necessary to consider another species of tortious causes of action, specifically misrepresentation.

Professional negligence

The most simple of duties – that to carry out the tasks entrusted to the professional adviser with the skill and care to be expected of a reasonably competent professional practising in that area. The authority in this area stretches back to Bolam v Friern Hospital Management Committee[15] and is well established as being the standard where the negligence of a professional is averred.

This gives rise to a duty on the firm, where it assumes such duty, to apply that degree of skill and care. However, the existence of a coextensive duty in tort parallel to the duties imposed in the Handbook has been firmly rejected in the Court of Appeal in Green and Rowley v RBS[16] and reaffirmed in CGL v RBS[17]. In the former case Tomlinson LJ considered that it would "drive a coach and horses through the intention of Parliament to confer a private law cause of action upon a limited class." This was explicitly endorsed in the latter case.

Insofar as a negligence action itself can be founded this must therefore be brought by reference to the expertise of a reasonably competent professional practising in the discipline and so rests heavily upon expert evidence as to the reasonable range of professional opinion.

15 [1957] 1 WLR 583

16 [2013] EWCA Civ 1197

17 [2017] EWCA Civ 1073

Montgomery v Lanarkshire[18]

Since this case of 2015 regarding the scope of a doctor's responsibility in obtaining informed consent, there has been the prospect that a new standard could be applied in the case of other professionals as an alternative to the Bolam test. This Montgomery test can be briefly stated as taking "reasonable care to ensure that the patient was aware of any material risks involved in any recommended treatment."[19]. This is distinct from the Bolam duty in that it is not the direct application of medical knowledge and skill but rather the provision of appropriate information to enable informed consent from the patient.

More recently the case of O'Hare v Coutts[20] considered whether such a duty could be applied to a financial adviser. In reliance upon O'Hare this question was raised in the Court of Appeal in Barker v Baxendale-Walker[21], a solicitors negligence case, in which the court declined to disapply the Bolam test as the proper test in that case. Avoiding the question of extension of Montgomery, the Court of Appeal determined that the advice given was the object of the application of professional skill and care by the solicitor; therefore any warning (which was found to be necessary) as to potential ineffectiveness was found to be part and parcel of that advice.

Barker has not however closed the door to this duty applying to financial professionals – where the object may be considered to be the purchase of a financial product – being subjected to the

18 [2015] UKSC 11

19 Barker v Baxendale-Walker [2017] EWCA Civ 2056

20 [2016] EWHC 2224 (QB)

21 (ibid.)

informed consent duty. Nor can it be ignored that the discussion in O'Hare drew significant similarities between the Montgomery approach and that in COBS, there is therefore scope to argue that the implementation of COBS should be informed by Montgomery.

Misrepresentation

In addition to the traditional negligence causes of action the nature of provision of financial services involves significant communication of facts. This exposes a financial services firm to the risk of making a negligent (or fraudulent) misrepresentation as to the facts preceding the contract being entered into. The Misrepresentation Act 1967 can therefore be useful in cases of negligent misrepresentation.

Hedley Byrne

In the context of communication between a business and its customer it is clear that the well known duty in Hedley Byrne v Heller – where a person with special skill applies that skill then a duty of care arises subject to knowledge that this will be relied upon – provides an alternative cause of action, notably distinct from misrepresentation.

In short, the duty is to provide information which is not misleading where there is reasonable expectation of reliance, and in the absence of an exclusion. This has been most recently helpfully summarised at p.64 of Property Alliance Group v RBS[22].

This is of particular import where, unlike in cases of ordinary salesmanship, there is a significant informational asymmetry

22 [2018] EWCA Civ 355

between the salesman (firm) and purchaser (client). The client can reasonably expect not to be misled.

Therefore when considering misrepresentation it is also pertinent to consider whether the same facts may give rise to this alternative case if the standard for misrepresentation is not met.

Fiduciary duty

Where the relevant defendant has a fiduciary relationship with the financial firm then the additional fiduciary duty to act in the client's best interests arises. This can enable equitable remedies, such as an account of profits or equitable compensation, as alternatives or adjuncts to damages.

Section 150/138D FSMA

This is a specific cause of action for qualifying persons, as defined in the Rights of Action Regulations, making breaches of the Handbook requirements directly actionable where the Handbook permits this – for obvious reasons parts of the Handbook which do not impose duties which are relevant to harm caused to consumers are not actionable by consumers. These are instead for the FCA to enforce.

Importantly for cases against financial professionals, the rules regarding the provision of advice and sales of investments (COB/COBS), insurance (ICOBS) and mortgages (MCOB) all provide causes of action for private persons.

Causation

Simple "but for"

At its heart it is necessary to consider the alternative being sought – and this is intertwined with the remedy sought as they are often the same – in short, is it said that the claimant would have done nothing or would they have undertaken an alternative transaction?

This echoes the idea that there is a distinction between "no transaction" cases and other cases. However, as to the doubt over this concept as SAAMCO has been considered carefully in BPE v Hughes-Holland, as to which see below.

Detailed analysis of this issue however has to follow proper instructions on the claimant's own perspective, or a clearly plead case as to loss. Either approach must be informed by an expert view as to the proper advice at the time by an expert who understands the standard of care – particularly as to the reasonable range of professional opinion.

It is not evidentially sufficient to take a client at their word as to what they would have done – although this is a key component of the case – it must also be considered in light of what was reasonably available to them and what a competent firm would have offered; the latter being matters which expert opinions are likely to be necessary to inform. Nor can a firm be expected to set out its view as to what was reasonable by way of an alternative or defence. A firm can however state (with objective contemporaneous material in support) what it would have been able to offer.

Importantly, it is necessary to look at the exact acts complained of. It can be tempting to rely upon an instance of written advice as pivotal when, in reality, the sales process itself was so defective as to be the more effective cause of the loss.

Given the multitude of individual potential causes of action, each of these needs to be examined from a causation perspective because any of the breaches may ultimately be the one which the case turns upon, and the measure of loss and law of causation may vary depending upon the cause of action.

SAAMCO and BPE v Hughes-Holland

The leading case in any case of economic loss is South Australia Asset Management Company v York Montague Ltd[23] ("SAAMCO") which addressed the causal extent of liability and especially the extent of professional liability where losses 'caused' (in the factual rather than legal sense) may involve issues outside the professionals remit. In SAAMCO the extent of the valuer's liability to the lender for overvaluation leading to significant losses when the market fell was determined on a broad basis but then limited to those losses which would have been incurred if the overvaluation had been correct. This led to the idea of the "SAAMCO cap" on damages.

Two circumstances were discussed in the Court of Appeal in SAAMCO, the "no transaction" case in which no transaction would have been entered into absent the matters complained of; and the "successful transaction" case.

The difficulties with the principles led to the issue being revisited. In BPE v Hughes-Holland[24] the High Court decided this in one

23 [1997] AC 191

24 [2014] UKSC 24

fashion, with the Court of Appeal taking a different view before the Supreme Court revisited the issue in detail.

The crux of the case was that monies were advanced and used in a fashion not envisaged by the claimant, but that the defendant solicitors had failed in amending the precedent used for the loan agreement so that the use to which the monies were put was permitted. The development was however, quite speculative. Initially Mr Gabriel (who preceded his trustee in bankruptcy Mr Hughes-Holland as claimant) was successful however his damages were capped at the best outcome possible had the advice been non-negligent.

On appeal the Court of Appeal took the view that the project at the heart of the claim was hopeless in any event and therefore the loss rested on the claimant's poor judgment.

The Supreme Court however explained that the decision in SAAMCO rested on two key matters:

1. the valuer owed no duty insofar as the lender's decision to lend was concerned – his duty was to provide a valuation; and

2. consequently whilst, 'but for' that negligent advice the money may not have been lent, his liability was only in respect of the advice regarding the security obtained (at pp.35-36 of Lord Sumption's speech).

Lord Sumption's analysis clarified that the "advice" and "information" labels used in SAAMCO were not ideal. However, in doing so it was made clear that where the "adviser" is only providing part of the material from which the decision will be made then the limited scope of responsibility would apply (pp.39-41). Contrasted with cases of true "advice" where the duty is to look at all the circumstances and guide the decision made by the client. At paragraph 44 there is helpful dicta that the spectrum between "advice" and "information" cases is likely to include financial and advisers being much more likely to be giving "advice" as opposed to conveyancers or valuers who more exemplify "information" cases.

The "SAAMCO cap" was dismissed as an imprecise way of explaining the extent of liability borne in "information" type cases.

Whilst the outcome of BPE v Hughes-Holland was unfavourable to Mr Hughes-Holland, the guidance provided was helpful. Particularly, in cases involving financial advisers, because such financial advisers were used as an example in contradistinction to conveyancers – i.e. that the advice given by a financial adviser is to actively undertake the advice given; rather than the advice of a conveyancer which merely enables a decision to be made by the client.

"Buyer's regret/remorse" cases

Upon full consideration of the occasional case it can become apparent that, whilst not the best option for the client the product was within the range of those which were suitable and no other default gives rise to an action. Pragmatically, such cases need to be identified at as early a stage as possible as the effort necessary to investigate a case fully can be significant.

This is not to say that whenever the allegation of buyer's remorse is raised it is an accurate label for the case – were this so the case would be susceptible to summary judgment – rather the need for a proper expert opinion as to the reasonable range of professional opinion available at the time of the relevant transaction becomes acute and the issue may ultimately be the one upon which the case stands or falls.

This does contrast with the "best product" issue in COB 5 discussed below and there is certainly a tension to resolve between the law and the application of a higher standard in the Handbook.

Market forces

Most readers will be acutely aware of the seismic shifts in the financial markets over the past two decades. Such turmoil has led to significant development in the law in this area.

One of the earlier cases demonstrates differing first instance and appellate views as to how market forces should be addressed – and particularly the need for financial professionals to properly consider their duty rather than relying upon past performance. In Rubenstein v HSBC[25] the court initially found that whilst HSBC may have failed in its duty to properly advise on investments, the losses were caused by unforeseeable events. The Court of Appeal took the opposite view on causation – proper advice would not have inflicted such loss (at p.118).

25 [2011] EWHC 2304 (QB) at first instance and [2012] EWCA Civ 1184 on appeal.

Heads of loss

Loss of capital

The simplest form of loss is the direct loss sustained by the claimant having invested money which has resulted in a crystallised loss. Such crystallisation can occur by, for example, winding up of a fund or sale of the asset.

Uncrystallised losses may accrue when it becomes impossible to dispose of an asset for example, where a fund is insolvent and no redemptions are being made whilst restructuring is ongoing.

The scope of the advice in question must always be considered to ensure that the correct loss is addressed. This was clarified in Emptage v FSCS[26] in which the adviser gave both regulated advice to take a mortgage (extending rather than reducing borrowings and on interest only terms) and general advice to use the significantly increased borrowings to invest in overseas property with a view to making a large capital return on sale. The FSCS ultimately upheld the claim but declined to pay the additional losses arising from the (unregulated) advice to invest in overseas real estate. The correct view was that the whole advice was indivisible and as such the whole loss could be recovered.

Loss of investment opportunity

Even if capital is not lost – for example if successful mitigation is undertaken – then the claimant may well have lost out on the opportunity to invest in a suitable investment which would have produced a return.

26 [2013] EWCA Civ 729

The simplest example would have been to retain such funds on deposit and in some cases this is the appropriate alternative for low risk, low volatility short term holdings.

More likely it is necessary to look at what the proper range of advice would have been and construct a suitable counterfactual to approximate the losses sustained by reason of being in the 'wrong' portfolio. As can easily be imagined this can lead to situations where parties are proffering contrasting counterfactuals which are advantageous to each other. The determination of loss in this case may need cogent explanation.

When constructing a counterfactual there are two distinct schools of thought: (1) whether the counterfactual uses indices as constituents; or (2) actual funds. The use of indices, where total return data is available, has the advantage that such indices are often used as benchmarks for funds in the relevant sector and so rather than taking a real fund's performance and whether it outperformed or underperformed the relevant benchmark, the benchmark itself is used. Real funds have the advantage of true performance data but the disadvantage of a collateral attack that a retrospective view allows the best fund in a sector to be chosen. This is a satellite issue and one which a judge must ultimately address but could provide a fertile ground for criticism of parties unable to make reasonable compromises to narrow the scope of the issue.

One useful alternative is the situation where the client has been persuaded to disinvest in order to make a different investment then the performance of that original investment may be the appropriate counterfactual. This can have some force where the range of proper advice included to undertake no changes to investments. This has the added advantage of not incurring additional fees or charges on restructuring.

Loss of preferential taxation or other status

Investments may often be wrapped in a product which provides additional tax or other benefits.

Hence it is often the case that ISAs are used as a vehicle for the first tranche of investible monies so as to secure the additional tax benefits. Bonds can also be used in a tax advantageous fashion as they can be structured to attract Capital Gains Tax rather than Income Tax, but in doing so tend to bear significant charges.

Pensions may be the more obvious example as growth within a pension fund is untaxed. Therefore unusual ideas such as drawing pension monies to invest warrant careful attention to discern why such an idea was selected.

Loss of opportunity to otherwise invest monies

Circumstances can arise were the client could have otherwise used monies which were invested to take advantage of a business opportunity. This may be rarer than taking an alternative financial product but perfectly feasible for business owners.

Such a case would require compelling evidence in respect of causation – particularly that the client would have invested in that particular opportunity and also how much could have been invested (if there was a limit as to what funding was needed for example); and how such funding would have been applied.

The other interesting evidential problem is the expert evidence (most cases at least forensic accountancy) to show how the alternative would have performed had the additional funding been available.

Remedies

Damages

Almost definitionally a financial services claim is a money claim for damages. It is hard to conceive of circumstances where money is not always able to restore the claimant's position.

One mitigation step which is not necessarily required is the pursuit of speculative litigation with its inherent risks. As will be readily gleaned from the issues thus far there are often multiple routes which may be taken to secure redress – for example see the Connaught Low Income Fund litigation[27] in which fund members are seeking redress against fund managers, whilst financial advisers may also be liable[28] there are clear alternatives in issue. However, when a firm raises, regarding mitigation, that another defendant 'should' be pursued first it may be necessary to consider carefully if such a clam is a reasonable step, or whether it is merely speculative.

Where there are liquid investments in issue then mitigation must rely upon reasonable and appropriate advice as to steps to be taken to mitigate loss. As ever, clear records must be kept of advice and how it is executed. It is trite to note that an expert witness could

27 [2014] EWHC 3619 (Comm)

28 Financial Ombudsman Service Decision DRN 1283111, for example

not also act as a financial adviser addressing mitigation to avoid the conflict arising by reason of their partiality[29].

Residual value of illiquid investments

Many cases arise where the ultimate investment has subsequently failed, whether by liquidation, external action, abandonment or otherwise, this can leave some property held by the client holding some value. For example in Asset Land Investment Plc v FCA[30] the ultimate investment was structured as parcels of overseas land – therefore even though a UCIS was found to exist the individual purchasers owned parcels of land.

Assessment of damages in such a case must factor in the value of that asset and, if there is a realistic prospects of realising that value what credit must be given for it.

There is some authority for the proposition that a court may make an interim assessment of damages in Deeny v Gooda Walker (No 3)[31] so as to resolve the dispute whilst deferring the final assessment of quantum to a later, certain date. This is only practical where there is a certain date by which any realisations will be final otherwise a court is unlikely to be persuaded to leave the matter open. If such an order is sought it must be noted that the interim award must be conservatively assessed.

29 CPR Part 35

30 [2017] UKSC 17

31 QBD (Comm), [1995] 1 WLR 1206

Limitation

Whilst this is an issue familiar to every litigator there are a few points to consider specifically in the context of financial services litigation. Firstly, that the different legal bases of claim each engage the law of limitation slightly differently.

Contractual causes of action arise upon the breach of contract; therefore the failure of one party to comply with its obligation may occur long before the client of the firm sustains loss.

Breach of statutory duty being a species of tort requires loss to accrue to complete the cause of action. Therefore until a client is committed to a transaction[32] no loss has accrued.

In contract, whilst a cause of action in negligence similarly cannot accrue until loss is sustained, and therefore runs from the same date when the client committed to the transaction causing loss, the alternative time limit under Section 14A Limitation Act 1980 is available.

> *"14A Special time limit for negligence actions where facts relevant to cause of action are not known at date of accrual.*
>
> *(1) This section applies to any action for damages for negligence, other than one to which section 11 of this Act applies, where the starting date for reckoning the period of limitation under subsection (4)(b) below falls after the date on which the cause of action accrued.*
>
> *(2) Section 2 of this Act shall not apply to an action to which this section applies.*

32 See Shore v Sedgwick [2008] EWCA Civ 863 at pp.31-33

(3) An action to which this section applies shall not be brought after the expiration of the period applicable in accordance with subsection (4) below.

(4) That period is either—

(a) six years from the date on which the cause of action accrued; or

(b) three years from the starting date as defined by subsection (5) below, if that period expires later than the period mentioned in paragraph (a) above.

(5) For the purposes of this section, the starting date for reckoning the period of limitation under subsection (4)(b) above is the earliest date on which the plaintiff or any person in whom the cause of action was vested before him first had both the knowledge required for bringing an action for damages in respect of the relevant damage and a right to bring such an action.

(6) In subsection (5) above "the knowledge required for bringing an action for damages in respect of the relevant damage" means knowledge both—

(a) of the material facts about the damage in respect of which damages are claimed; and

(b) of the other facts relevant to the current action mentioned in subsection (8) below.

(7) For the purposes of subsection (6)(a) above, the material facts about the damage are such facts about the damage as would lead a reasonable person who had suffered such damage

to consider it sufficiently serious to justify his instituting proceedings for damages against a defendant who did not dispute liability and was able to satisfy a judgment.

(8) The other facts referred to in subsection (6)(b) above are—

(a) that the damage was attributable in whole or in part to the act or omission which is alleged to constitute negligence; and

(b) the identity of the defendant; and

(c) if it is alleged that the act or omission was that of a person other than the defendant, the identity of that person and the additional facts supporting the bringing of an action against the defendant.

(9) Knowledge that any acts or omissions did or did not, as a matter of law, involve negligence is irrelevant for the purposes of subsection (5) above.

(10) For the purposes of this section a person's knowledge includes knowledge which he might reasonably have been expected to acquire—

(a) from facts observable or ascertainable by him; or

(b) from facts ascertainable by him with the help of appropriate expert advice which it is reasonable for him to seek; but a person shall not be taken by virtue of this subsection to have knowledge of a fact ascertainable only with the help of expert advice so long as he has taken all reasonable steps to obtain (and, where appropriate, to act on) that advice."

This has been, unsurprisingly, a hotly contested provision as it can enable an action to be brought up to 15 years (as such a long-stop is imposed in s.14B) after accrual.

The running of time from the first date upon which constructive knowledge sufficient to alert the client to begin investigations is key. This standard was fixed at that level in Haward v Fawcetts[33], in the words of Lord Nicholls, "the claimant must know enough for it to be reasonable to begin to investigate further." This principle has been upheld in, inter alia, Jacobs v Sesame[34], and Shore v Sedgwick[35] in the context of financial services claims.

It should also be noted that the provisions of section 32 Limitation Act 1980, where there has been deceit or concealment of facts material to the cause of action[36], are available in financial services cases; however, the evidence necessary must be considered carefully as such allegations of deceit are subject to the weighing of the seriousness of the allegation when considering the probabilities[37].

33 [2006] UKHL 9

34 [2014] EWCA Civ 1410

35 [2008] EWCA Civ 863

36 For a synopsis of the caselaw Arcadia Group v Visa [2015] EWCA Civ 883 is detailed in its consideration.

37 Re H (Minors) (Sexual Abuse: Standard of Proof) [1996] AC 563

CHAPTER THREE
THE HANDBOOK

In ascertaining liability the preeminent source of allegations can be found in the rules which a financial professional is expected to comply with – the FCA Handbook – or more specifically the suitability or appropriateness regimes found in the Conduct of Business Sourcebook (COBS).

The predecessor regime of COB ("Conduct of Business") which was replaced effective 1 November 2009, and is addressed by contrast to the present COBS regime. Although it should be noted that such claims are likely subject to limitation issues.

COBS

COBS 2

The core Principles of "Treating Customers Fairly" (Principle 6) and communicating in a manner which is "clear, fair and not misleading" (Principle 7) are not directly actionable for breach.

Therefore to enable enforceable requirements these concepts are recast in COBS 2.1.1 R and COBS 2.2.1 R; and at COBS 4.2.

In COBS 2.1.1 R a duty to treat customers fairly is imposed in very broad terms and so can formulate a broad basis for claims, if proper particulars of breach can be advanced. This is a useful residual duty where other elements of the regulatory framework fail to express a rule but guidance or common sense dictate that a duty should exist.

COBS 2.2.1 R mandates that information about the firm, what it does and how it charges must be provided to the client. This is permitted to be provided in a standardised form, hence does not need to be tailored to the client but it must be sufficient to enable the client to make informed choices.

COB 2 (prior to 1 November 2011)

The direct ancestor to the COBS 2 provisions can be found at COB 2. These are practically very similar to COBS and were not significantly rewritten.

COBS 4.2 Fair, clear and not misleading

Principle 7 is restated in actionable form at COBS 4.2.1 R (1) along with guidance at COBS 4.2.4 G to set out in more detail how a firm can achieve this aim.

Note, there is an exceptional defence of reasonable steps at COBS 4.2.6 R, however the burden in such a case is on the firm to show that it has taken reasonable steps.

COBS 4 Financial Promotions

The mere distribution of material promoting financial products is restricted – pursuant to s.21 FSMA – and the steps of preparing and approving such promotions fall within this scope. The precise extent is set out in The Financial Services and Markets Act 2000 (Financial Promotion) Order 2001[1] (the "Financial Promotion

1 SI 2001/1335

Order"), specifically at Article 5, and the Financial Promotion Order sets out the various exemptions.

However, the rules in relation to are set down in COBS 4. These rules extend to all forms of financial promotion – from billboards and newspaper advertisements through to the prospectus and offering document for a specialist fund.

One important restriction, but not outright prohibition, is on cold calling at COBS 4.8.2 R which sets very clear limits on what can be done by way of a cold call.

Key information is required to be supplied: so that the promotion is clearly identifiable as a financial promotion (COBS 4.3) and information about any compensation scheme is limited to a factual reference only (COBS 4.4).

There are more detailed requirements at COBS 4.5.2 R (et seq.) as to what a firm must comply with carefully when communicating with retail clients, particularly regarding a balanced presentation of issues. When communicating regarding performance rules at COBS 4.5A and COBS 4.6 are engaged and set stringent requirements to ensure that such communications are not improper.

More generally, direct offer financial promotions are addressed in COBS 4.7. Broadly, such a promotion is an open invitation to the public to engage in regulated business and sets out the requirements necessary to do so.

Certain regulated investments attract additional protections, at COBS 4.7.6 R any financial promotion in relation to warrants or derivatives may not be approved or communicated without ensuring that COBS 10 appropriateness will be complied with – and in awareness that the client may be responding to a direct offer financial promotion.

Direct offer financial promotions in relation to non-readily realisable securities to retail clients are much more significantly restricted by COBS 4.7.7 R – 4.7.10 R. Specifically requiring pre-existing certificates as to the status of the client to receive such promotions and the obligations on the firm who will ultimately deal with the response to the promotion.

At COBS 4.12 R (formerly COB 3 Annex 5 R) the rules restricting promotion of non-mainstream pooled investments, parallel to the statutory restrictions in the PCIS Order, can be found. Notably, COBS 4.12.4 R includes a slightly broader scope of recipients of promotions, giving rise to a certain tension between the legal and regulatory position.

COB 3 (prior to 1 November 2011)

The translation of the rules on financial promotions from COB 3 to COBS 4 did not entail significant revisions however, as these rules all evolved over time it is vital to refer to the relevant rules as in force at the time.

<u>COBS 9 Suitability</u>

This applies (per COBS 9.1.1 R) to the activities of giving a personal recommendation (Art. 53 RAO) and (per COBS 9.1.3 R) managing investments (Art. 37 RAO) in relation to designated investments.

In order for a financial professional to give such a personal recommendation or make a decision to trade under a discretionary mandate, COBS 9.2 and 9.3 set out the requirements which a financial professional must comply with in order to establish that the recommendation or decision is suitable.

Each of the prescribed issues must be taken in turn and addressed sequentially so as to build up a proper assessment of the client. In practice it can be seen that such questions are not always clearly addressed individually but careful consideration must be given to whether the firm satisfied the information gathering requirement. This is important as, once facts are ascertained they must be considered together to enable the client to be advised as to how their demands can be best met within the constraints of their needs and attitude to risk.

It is possible for an adviser to agree with their client not to consider certain issues – such as a pre-existing buy-to-let property portfolio – when giving advice but in obtaining instructions to exclude certain matters must explain the basis for this and enable the client to make an informed choice. In the example of a client with an extensive buy-to-let property portfolio comprising a major part of a client's wealth a financial adviser is likely to recommend disinvestment in order to ensure that the asset allocation of investments across sectors is not heavily skewed towards property. Therefore will suffer more in the event of a downturn in the property market (howsoever caused); as such disinvestment is unlikely then a properly set out warning and waiver will enable the firm and client to proceed ignoring that aspect of the client's assets.

If a client refuses to provide information then the adviser may advise as best they can provided that such advice is appropriately caveated. However, per COBS 9.2.4 R the firm is prohibited from encouraging information not to be supplied.

Many advisory and discretionary management relationships are long-term and as such, a client's circumstances may change significantly. To avoid the risk of incorrect advice or exercise of discretion an adviser must avoid relying upon stale information per COBS 9.2.5 R.

For the purposes of retrospectively considering advice it is necessary to consider these issues at the time of sale. A proper exercise of discretion also requires (COBS 9.5) that the adviser maintains a record of the information gathered and relied upon for the purposes of that advice or exercise of discretion. Often this will be restated in a suitability letter as the firm is required to set its advice in writing in accordance with COBS 9.4.1 R; but to investigate a claim may require disclosure on the part of the firm to obtain this information.

These are not set out in prescriptive detail because the Handbook is intended to be outcomes focused – therefore the exact steps taken to effect compliance with its requirements are up to the financial services firm in question.

In order to demonstrate compliance with COBS 9 it can readily be observed that a financial professional must have taken steps:

1. to investigate the client's circumstances;
2. to consider the available products;
3. to provide clear and coherent advice to the client as to what is recommended; and

4. to justify that advice by reference to the first two points.

It is important to note that the client is not presumed to be unintelligent or uninvolved.

There is often a life changing sum of money involved and therefore the client will often be keenly interested and distinguishing reconstruction and overthinking from what is recorded contemporaneously can present a challenge. As a matter of evidence the discussion of the fallibility of human memory in Gestmin SA v Credit Suisse[2] has been approved at the highest level in R (on the application of Bancoult No 3) v Secretary of State for Foreign and Commonwealth Affairs[3].

Cases have addressed judicial comments as to suitability, and the ultimate determination made by the court. Notably, however, these do not purport to set out at any time a definitive approach to be taken. A broad selection of such cases include:

- Worthing v Lloyds
- Jacobs v Sesame
- Rubenstein v HSBC
- O'Hare v Coutts

(all being cited elsewhere)

Ultimately, it cannot be forgotten that determination of the suitability of the advice given is a question of fact for a court and

2 [2013] EWHC 3560 (Comm)

3 [2018] UKSC 3

must be treated as such. The caselaw demonstrates an ongoing tension between judges who feel comfortable addressing the application of COBS, it being the mere implementation of a European legal instrument, as a matter of construction for the court; against those who view it as the exercise of professional skill necessitating the useful opinion of an expert witness. Whatever the view taken by the court under Part 35, it would be unwise to second guess suitability without guidance from an expert.

Insistent clients

As suggested above it is possible for a firm to provide financial services which may at first glance appear unsuitable. The most common such circumstance is when the firm is faced with an insistent client who wishes to undertake a particular transaction even when advised not to do so.

This possibility should not be abused by a firm which, on paper advises against a product, but orally encourages a client to undertake an unsuitable transaction.

This option must be considered carefully by a firm as it is perfectly permissible to earn fees for undertaking work which is unsuitable for the client. When employed it should be supported by the clearest of evidence that the advice was properly conveyed to the client and that the client understood properly the nature and effect of proceeding against the advice.

From an objective standpoint, where the fee earned varies dependent upon whether advice was followed or not can lead to the suggestion that a firm has a financial motivation to close a sale. Where there is no difference in the remuneration received this can significantly strengthen the use of this arrangement.

COB 5 (pre 1 November 2011)

The rules in COBS 9 derive heavily from those set out in COB 5 and the provisions at COB 5.2, 5.3 and 5.4 are clear ancestors in similar terms to the COBS 9 rules.

One notable rule which was not reprised in COBS is COB 5.3.5 R (2) – which requires advice not to transact to be given where none of the packaged products available are the best product. This distinction may seem trivial however such a restriction is important in ensuring that firms are careful regarding selection of options and, particularly where commissions varied based upon the recommendation given, that advice is the best available.

That "best product" rule was not followed through to COBS. Nevertheless it is not a distant leap to assert that Principle 6 (client's best interests) requires that where the product being offered is not the best – and not just the best available to the adviser to sell – that the client should be made aware that there are better products available elsewhere.

COBS 10 Appropriateness

Certain financial products attract a greater degree of protection when COBS 9 suitability is not engaged – for example in execution only sales. This only applied originally to derivatives and warrants, but from 1 April 2014 widened to include all non-readily realisable investments (as defined in the Handbook's Glossary). By this definition, mainstream regulated investments such as shares traded on a main market do not engage this additional layer of protection.

The crux of the requirements (COBS 10.2.1 R) are to establish the client's knowledge of the risk involved in the product is sufficient. To do so COBS 10.2.2 R sets out a non exclusive list of issues to be inquired about, with further guidance under COBS 10.5; and COBS 10.2.3 R imposes a bar on discouraging the client from providing information.

Where the firm considers the transaction inappropriate this must be communicated (COBS 10.3.1 R) in the form of a warning. However, per COBS 10.3.3 G the firm must consider whether it wishes to proceed with the inappropriate transaction once the warning is given.

There are certain specific exemptions at COBS 10.4 to the need to undertake appropriateness testing.

Restricted advice

One development which has been severely deprecated by the FCA[4] is the giving of advice limited to only part of a proposed transaction – particularly the use of a wrapper such as a SIPP. This was exemplified when the FCA took action against the principals of 1 Stop[5] for purporting to provide advice on a pension transfer only whilst denying any involvement in the 'real' transaction of investing into wholly unsuitable, high risk and esoteric schemes. On the face of it such advice seemed to legitimately exclude any consideration of the underlying investments and only addressed the target SIPP which was cheapest to set up on the presumption that the client wished to undertake the transaction in any event.

---

4 https://www.fca.org.uk/news/news-stories/pension-transfers-or-switches-view-investing-pension-monies-unregulated-products

5 https://www.fca.org.uk/publication/final-notices/timothy-adrian-hughes.pdf

More broadly, Emptage v FSCS[6] addressed the advice given by her mortgage adviser to Mrs Emptage in which the adviser developed an idea involving (regulated) mortgage advice and the (unregulated) idea of extending Mrs Emptage's mortgage on her home to invest in real estate in Spain. The FSCS originally awarded just losses relating to the mortgage itself and not those additional losses arising out of the real estate speculation in Spain. The Court of Appeal disagreed and held that the entire advice was indivisible and the adviser was responsible for it all, therefore the FSCS was also responsible for all of it.

Importantly – and particularly post-RDR where advice appears expensive – these criticisms of poor advisory processes do not detract from the ability of an adviser to genuinely consider only a limited scope of advice and deliver a proper service.

Execution only business

There are many circumstances where a firm may be employed solely to bring about a transaction without considering the merits. The archetypical example would be a stockbroker who merely effects the share transaction sought by their client.

There are also circumstances where what appears to be execution only business in fact involves a degree of persuasion or recommendation and careful consideration may need to be given as to what actually occurred.

6 [2013] EWCA Civ 729

"Introducing"

The introducing only position is a simple circumstance where the introducer purports to give no specific advice, merely instead informing the client about the product in question and earning a commission on the sale when the client purchases the product.

Notably an unregulated person may seek to rely upon the exemption in article 33 RAO to act as an *introducer* of financial products provided they comply strictly with the terms of that exemption. This is particularly important since this article provides an exemption only to *arranging* (article 25 RAO) and the definition of *arranging* is very broad as set out in Personal Touch Financial Services v SimplySure[7]. That breadth allows arranging to be more easily established and, this is construed as intentional so that the only exemptions available are the explicit ones, such as for communications providers and introducers.

The introducing exemption to arranging is clearly defined:

> *"33. There are excluded from articles 25(2), 25A(2), 25B(2), 25C(2) and 25E(2) arrangements where—*
>
> *(a) they are arrangements under which persons ("clients") will be introduced to another person;*
>
> *(b) the person to whom introductions are to be made is—*
>
> *(i) an authorised person;*
>
> *(ii) an exempt person acting in the course of a business comprising a regulated activity in relation to which he is exempt; or*

7 [2016] EWCA Civ 461

(iii) a person who is not unlawfully carrying on regulated activities in the United Kingdom and whose ordinary business involves him in engaging in an activity of the kind specified by any of articles 14, 21, 25, 25A, 25B, 25C, 25E, 37, 39A, 40, 45, 51, 52, 53, 53A, 53B, 53C and 53D (or, so far as relevant to any of those articles, article 64), or would do so apart from any exclusion from any of those articles made by this Order;

(c) the introduction is made with a view to the provision of independent advice or the independent exercise of discretion in relation to investments generally or in relation to any class of investments to which the arrangements relate; and

(d) the arrangements are made with a view to a person entering into a transaction which does not relate to a contract of insurance."

Crucially therefore, where there is no advice to be given (or discretion to be exercised) by the regulated firm the exemption cannot be engaged, even if the client is introduced to a business which is providing other financial services lawfully.

This exemption for *introducing* gives rise to the possibility of unregulated company as an introducer to profitability effect sales by their very nature being unregulated and benefiting from the absence of regulatory burden that operating such a business entails.

Dealing with such cases raises issues as to whether advice was actually provided, and if so whether an otherwise unregulated business also breached the general prohibition needs to be considered carefully to properly formulate a case.

A second exemption is available at Art. 29 for dealing through an authorised person but this prohibits the 'introducer' from taking any fee or other remuneration other than directly from the client, and no advice has been given by the 'introducer'. This is quite restricted in its scope and commercially not very useful.

CHAPTER FOUR
REGULATED INVESTMENTS

These come in a number of common varieties, often involving stocks and shares, packaged products, structured products, ISAs, investment bonds etc. These are addressed previously in general terms but as each one has its own peculiarities they warrant a brief discussion to enable clear identification and to highlight potential issues.

Funds

One of the most common constituents in a portfolio of any sort is the fund. This allows an individual investor access to a much greater breadth of investments and the professional management of that portfolio than would be achievable at a reasonable cost to the small investor.

For example, an individual keen to invest in FTSE100 companies may attempt to:

i. build a portfolio tracking the composition of the FTSE100;

ii. pick example FTSE100 shares from each industry;

iii. invest in a 'tracker' fund which is a simple fund whose management does nothing but maintain a proportionate holding in the entire FTSE100 basket of shares; or

iv. invest in a fund whose manager has a remit of working with FTSE100 shares but outperforming the index.

Funds do not just invest in shares, funds investing in bonds and property are also very common. More esoteric funds can be found, including hedge funds which can vary wildly in their approach and target investors.

Funds can be found which invest across diverse asset, geographic, industry and market capitalisation classes and can therefore provide exposure to diverse classes at modest investment levels.

For a modest portfolio, funds can provide access to asset classes which could not otherwise be reached. For example, investing in emerging markets may be a suitable part of a portfolio, but an English financial adviser may be hard pressed to recommend individual shares across four different economies and the whole range of industries, whereas selecting an emerging markets fund can be done relatively simply by comparing the performance of fund managers in this area.

Exchange Traded Funds

The funds previously discussed are operated by large financial institutions with access to significant internal resources to establish and trade. An ETF, or exchange traded fund, is an investment fund wrapped in a company structure so that it can be publicly listed on an exchange. The ETF is an evolution of that concept to enable a fund to raise money directly from anyone able to trade on the relevant stock exchange.

Dealing Cost

Direct investment in individual financial instruments carries a cost which is not proportionate to value. That is, a dealing fee is likely to be fixed, or taper off in larger value transactions. Thus, when looking at a recommendation it may be necessary to consider if the cost of implementing the advice may result in it not being the most suitable recommendation.

This ability to invest one sum into a fund rather than a dozen smaller transactions enables the fixed costs of dealing to be paid once rather than, say, a dozen times thereby effecting access to a more diverse portfolio at reduced cost.

The cost of transacting in funds may also be demonstrated as a bid/offer spread, that being the difference between the price at which units can be bought compared to the price at which they can be sold.

Stocks and Shares

These are defined quite simply in Art. 76 RAO.

Notably, provided they are listed on a recognised exchange these are considered liquid, or readily realisable and therefore do not attract the additional protections of COBS 10.

As an investment type, shares can vary in the level of risk attached; however, individual shares are generally regarded as reasonably high risk as they are wholly dependent upon the fortunes of a single company.

Derivatives

Derivatives (certain of which are defined in articles 83 – 85 RAO) are significantly more complex contractual arrangements which come in various varieties. They were originally developed as instruments to enable those involved in financial markets to "hedge" positions or take a speculative position which they could not do without effecting significant equity transactions.

The typical example from an investments context are contracts for differences ("CFDs"). From a 'protection' perspective swaps are a common example.

Derivatives are usually sold as over the counter ("OTC") products with the counterparty being the bank or platform provider. This raises one initial issue which is that the only rates and terms available once tied to such a platform are those offered by that platform.

CFDs

The most common derivative being the CFD, they can be focused upon. Swaps are addressed separately. CFDs are a tax efficient way of speculating on movement of prices of the underlying asset (traded commodities, shares, even indices); as they do not attract the duties which apply to effecting an actual purchase. These also allow 'short' positions to be taken – that being an intention to profit on a fall in value, which could (in the example of shares) only otherwise be done by selling options (another derivative) at a fixed price with a view to actually acquiring the deliverable shares at a later date and lower price. A 'long' position – that the share will rise – avoids the stamp duty attached to the purchase.

These are defined as "contractually based obligations" in the RAO as they consist of a bundle of contractual rights between client and counterparty. The primary obligation on each side being to pay the balance due upon closing out of the contract, the payer depending upon which direction the value of the underlying asset has changed.

Two major issues are margin and leverage. Margin reflects the assets (usually cash, but can be security over land/assets in the case of interest rate hedging products) held by the trading platform provider against adverse changes in the value of such derivatives as are held at any given instant by the client. Therefore if a client has six open positions and two are positive but four are negative the margin required to be held would be that which is sufficient to terminate (either paying or receiving depending on if each is positive or negative) all six positions and still leave a non-negative balance against the cash account.

Leverage can allow the derivative instrument to multiply the gain or loss attributable to it. This can be advantageous because for a low commitment of cash potentially significant gains can be made. However, losses are also magnified. As is the requisite margin.

These two issues come together[1] when a client's net position turns against them and the platform provider calls for additional margin funds. The provider will require that the margin held is sufficient to pay any sums due if the market moves against the client.

This is pivotal because if the asset underlying a CFD drops in value then if the client does not hold enough margin and is unwilling to pay more cash by way of margin then the counter-

1 For an example of margin calls see Zaki v Credit Suisse [2012] EWCA Civ 583

party can close out the transaction and the client's margin is used to pay the sum due to the counterparty.

Often CFDs are subject to stop loss provisions. These work so that once a certain loss would be realised the counterparty will automatically close the transaction and the loss be incurred but curtailed. This cannot however be guaranteed in turbulent market conditions.

Swaps

Swaps and interest rate hedging products ("IRHPs") are not synonymous. Rather, IRHPs are instances of swaps.

At its heart a swap is relatively simple – two streams of income by reference to one principal sum are swapped.

Therefore in the case of interest rate swaps an (almost invariably – however not absolutely necessary) fixed rate on an agreed principal sum is swapped with a (almost invariably) floating rate on the same principal sum by reference to a defined base rate, tenor and period. These do not need to relate to any particular loan and can even be entered for speculative purposes.

These are useful as between market counterparties who wish to control their exposure to fixed rates – and their trading partners who wish to speculate against them, or are willing to take on the risk for a fee.

As these involve a commitment over time which can be relied upon as an outgoing or incoming and so financial projections made upon the basis of it these have a spot value – that is what would it cost to purchase a swap to exactly negate the remaining obligation; or what profit could be realised by selling the swap on. It is this point which makes a swap a wholly different creature to a fixed rate mortgage (where the costs of early repayment or termination are fixed, or at least the basis of calculation is fixed, at the outset). If – as happened in the late 2000s – financial markets take an unprecedented turn then the cost of breaking the swap can become significantly more than was realistically foreseeable at the outset.

It should be remembered that such swaps are done by reference to an agreed base rate (Bank of England, a bank rate or one of the various tenors of LIBOR for example) and the margin payable to the lender is unaffected.

One notable oddity is currency rate swaps in which the principal currency sum is actually transferred between the parties, presumably because the value of that principal can change significantly during the course of the contract and therefore each party needs further protection against such movements.

Other IRHPs

All other interest rate hedging products are, at heart a sort of cap and can be explained as forms of swap. A cap is a simple agreement in which, for a premium, if a floating rate interest payment obligation (with respect to a principal, tenor and period) reaches a certain level then the counterparty will pay the interest due above that capped level.

Commercially it can therefore be expected that the higher the cap level (further for base rates to reach) and the shorter the period it is in place for (therefore more predictable rates are) then the lower the premium would be.

The reverse of a cap is a floor. This imposes a floor on the interest rate payable. So if interest rates fall dramatically then, whilst a floating rate would drop with it, this would halt the drop and the customer would pay the counterparty the difference between the floor rate and the floating rate. Much as a customer would pay a premium for a cap, a counterparty would expect to pay the customer for taking out a floor.

The floor may appear strange at first glance but it is the second part of a collar and is used by a counterparty offering a cap to reduce the up-front premium for the cap by imposing a limit below which the counterparty will earn rather than pay if interest rates fall significantly.

These basic components were used to build the "structured collar" which, unlike a regular collar, may allow for more complex swapping of rates; for example if the floor rate were reached by the relevant base rate, the rate which is payable by the client may be greater than that floor rate.

IRHP claims

At the time of writing, the FCA Review of IRHPs has concluded and the vast majority of litigation in relation to them has also resolved, particularly the satellite litigation in CGL v RBS referred to above.

For completeness, it is necessary to briefly explain why they were unsuitable. The short view however is that there was at the time no retail market in IRHPs – therefore when a lender insisted on such 'protection' that the IRHP would be invariably purchased from the lender (or a related institution). As there was no open market in these products it was very difficult to obtain accurate pricing information to ascertain if the product being sold was properly priced.

The major problem with disputes over these sales was the exclusion of advisory duties by major lenders when dealing with businesses who do not attract private person status. This led to the Green & Rowley v RBS and CGL v RBS cases finding against the customer on, respectively, concurrent COBS duties in tort and assumption of COBS duties in undertaking the FCA Review of IRHPs.

Hidden credit lines are a logical issue which arise when considering that the counterparty is a secured lender, and that lender has a broadly phrased charge over the borrower's assets. Since the IRHP appears on the lender/counterparty's books it must have a value either being classed as secured or not, therefore on date of sale a value needs to be ascribed to it and updated as the markets move; therefore as IRHP appears on the counterparty/lender's books for the purposes of capital adequacy having it's book value within the security held against the borrower may be advantageous. However, this means that the lender often could book significant immediate profit and did not disclose this liability which the borrower had to it – that value being effectively the breakage cost of the IRHP at any given valuation date.

The sales tactics sometimes involved the introduction late in the secured lending process of the requirement for 'interest rate protection' (or a similar phrase); often after a sufficient offer of lending to commit the borrower to the purchase. Then a salesman, described as an adviser but not acting as an adviser, would sell a vision of the future of rising rates (which may not necessarily accord with the lender's own view – evidenced by the market valuation of the IRHPs) and then selling collars, structured collars and swaps; in many cases not matched well to the underlying borrowing.

Bonds

Defined in articles 77 (private debt) & 78 (government debt) RAO these are a debt instrument entitling the bondholder to payment of the principal sum borrowed upon maturity and, in the meantime often a regular interest payment (sometimes referred to as a coupon).

Bonds can be issued by governments (often referred to as gilts or treasury bonds) or large publicly limited companies. Such bonds may also be traded.

Untraded bonds also exist, and may be a smaller issue or a private issue. Mini-bonds are a subspecies of these which allow even small enterprises to issue bonds without the significant requirements imposed upon bonds which are tradeable.

Crowdfunding platforms may use a mini-bond structure to raise funds rather than a sale of equity.

As a debt instrument a bond is only as strong as its issuer, therefore even if the issuer is a country there can be a default risk (for example, the Russian GKO as involved in Springwell Navigation v JP Morgan Chase[2]).

2 [2005] EWCA Civ 1602

Deposits

Defined in article 5 RAO these are exactly what they sound like. However, deposits are not held on trust. On the contrary the deposited funds are a debt owed by the deposit taker to the depositor.

It must be remembered that deposit taking is a specific activity requiring specific permissions and also attracting capital adequacy requirements.

There is no obligation on the deposit taker to pay interest but a power to do so. It is because of the breadth of Article 5(2)(a) that structured products (below) were designed in deposit terms in some circumstances.

Structured Products

Structured products are instruments designed to provide a degree of certainty with a prospect of enhanced returns. They can be structured as contractually based investments or – in a way which may avoid designated investment status – as deposits. These were often sold as "guaranteed investments" or other such phrases indicating certainty.

The crux of such products is exposing the investor to gains referable to an index, shares or some other higher risk investment whilst offering the certainty of return of capital provided the product is held to maturity. Such products are therefore clearly alternatives to fixed term deposits and fixed term investment bonds; however such other fixed term products tend to carry certainty of return. The other tradeoff would be a limit on the returns achievable by, for example, achieving a certain level and then the product winding up early and paying out.

Whilst apparently paradoxical in offering better returns with the certainty of return of capital these seem at first glance potentially very good for consumers. The reality of such structured products is, as set out by the FCA in TR 15/02, that such products were not easily understandable by consumers, and returns were overestimated frequently.

Life insurance

Life insurance bonds are sometimes used as a wrapper for other investments to enable an investor to access the funds operated by the life office. Therefore if an investor wishes to invest in a large insurer's particular property fund they may not be able to access this other than through a policy issued by the life office.

These often also provide access to funds supermarkets mentioned above.

These may also include an element of underwritten life insurance, however, the event of death of the insured is often merely a means of effecting surrender. That mechanism does allow such a policy to be written in trust. The current taxation of partial surrender of such a policy allows a limited amount of the value invested to be drawn annually without accruing a liability to tax; importantly, the applicable tax regime is that of capital gains, therefore whilst the use of this wrapper may appear expensive at the outset, these can be deployed to reduce net exposure to tax.

Pensions

Pensions are regulated under multiple regimes, not all of which are within the remit of the FCA and/or PRA.

Many activities in relation to stakeholder pension schemes have been regulated under the RAO since 2001 (Art. 82 defining such pensions). All personal pension schemes were brought into scope as "securities" by amendment of Art. 82 effective 6 April 2007[3].

The issues particular to pensions are considered below.

Non-mainstream Pooled Investments / Unregulated Collective Investment Schemes

These two investment types (being virtually synonymous) refer to a veritable smorgasbord of interesting products. To properly characterise these the definition of a collective investment scheme can be found at section 235 of FSMA:

> *"235 Collective investment schemes*
>
> *(1) In this Part "collective investment scheme" means any arrangements with respect to property of any description, including money, the purpose or effect of which is to enable persons taking part in the arrangements (whether by becoming owners of the property or any part of it or otherwise) to participate in or receive profits or income arising from the acquisition, holding, management or disposal of the property or sums paid out of such profits or income.*

3 SI 2006/1969

(2) The arrangements must be such that the persons who are to participate ("participants") do not have day-to-day control over the management of the property, whether or not they have the right to be consulted or to give directions.

(3) The arrangements must also have either or both of the following characteristics—

(a) the contributions of the participants and the profits or income out of which payments are to be made to them are pooled;

(b) the property is managed as a whole by or on behalf of the operator of the scheme.

(4) If arrangements provide for such pooling as is mentioned in subsection (3)(a) in relation to separate parts of the property, the arrangements are not to be regarded as constituting a single collective investment scheme unless the participants are entitled to exchange rights in one part for rights in another.

(5) The Treasury may by order provide that arrangements do not amount to a collective investment scheme—

(a) in specified circumstances; or

(b) if the arrangements fall within a specified category of arrangement."

Importantly this prescribes no form or requirement of a collective investment scheme save that it comprises "arrangements". This is a very broad term as expounded by the Supreme Court in Asset

Land Investment v FCA[4] and can include multiple separate elements amounting between them to the arrangements. For example, the sale of land and subsequent contracts for management were found in that case to bring together all of the elements necessary to be arrangements.

The promotion of such schemes is prohibited by section 238 and so it is necessary for narrower and specific exemptions for those categories of collective investment schemes which may be lawfully promoted. There are the approved types of scheme within section 238 of FSMA:

1. authorised unit trusts (defined in s.237);
2. authorised collective investment schemes (defined in s.236);
3. recognised schemes (per ss. 264, 270 or 272); and
4. the Treasury may make further orders under s.235(5) excluding the prohibition.

Such further orders include The Financial Services and Markets Act 2000 (Collective Investment Schemes) Order 2001[5] (the "CIS Order").

Or, arrangements may be determined not to amount to a collective investment scheme at all. For example, paragraph 21 of the schedule to the CIS Order, defines that a trading company (that is not an open ended investment company) does not amount to a collective investment scheme, as otherwise their shares would be a clear example of units a collective investment scheme.

4 [2016] UKSC 17

5 SI 2001/1062

For the purposes of the regulation of financial services, it is necessary to note that the definition of an unregulated collective investment scheme is a subset of collective investment schemes. Therefore, pursuant to Article 83 RAO, because units in a collective investment scheme are a designated investment (to which activities including dealing as a principal, dealing as an agent, arranging deals in and advising upon are regulated activities) these are brought within the scope of the regulatory framework – and all the consequences thereof.

Mortgages

Mortgages, being borrowing products, are somewhat different in the approach which must be taken.

Similar provisions to those applicable to other products:

1. provision of information
2. commission disclosures
3. affordability checking

These appear to be simple to comply with but failures do lead to unsuitable sales, particularly where an interest only loan is sold coupled with (however loosely) an investment product intended to pay off the capital sum.

The mis-selling of these is however a specialist and technical subject beyond the scope of this book.

CHAPTER FIVE ISSUES PARTICULAR TO PORTFOLIOS

Whilst above individual investments are considered and suitability is discussed in the context of individual advice, lurking in the background to suitability is the client's whole set of circumstances. Often when looking at assets and liabilities this will include a client's home, mortgage and pension arrangements which are often in place with little or no prior advice. A more complex individual in later life may have a second home, shares acquired through bonus schemes or as a result of individual speculation and ISA arrangements. These, whilst they may not appear to be classical portfolios, amount to a portfolio of investments and liabilities which need to be borne in mind by a careful adviser.

When considering a client's circumstances and the proper composition of a portfolio of investments it can be necessary to advise and warn as to over-exposure to (for example) property in the case of a small buy-to-let landlord; this, when properly warned can allow the client to exclude a significant property exposure from the advice being given.

Such a step is necessary to enable an adviser to proceed to advise without the first step being to divest assets which the client does not wish (for their own reasons) to divest. This would typically lead to advice which would be prima facie unsuitable as overexposed to (in this example) property.

A modern adviser has access to many tools provided by major investment houses to compose a suitable portfolio reflecting the fact finding undertaken by the adviser and input to such a tool. Some leeway can often be found based on a client's preferences but such a tool, properly used, will direct a suitable portfolio of investments.

Alternatively, if such investigations are done manually, then model portfolios are defined by the Wealth Managers Association (WMA, formerly APCIMS) aimed at different objectives and risk profiles and giving appropriate asset allocations by reference to major indices to allow an adviser to select within an asset class appropriate investments.

Ongoing advice v Individual sales

Many adviser's terms are directed to a one off instance of advice, and any subsequent advice is at the request of the client. This is not unusual for individual sales but care must be taken to ensure that such terms reflect the commercial reality of an adviser's relationship with its client.

This was particularly common pre-RDR in that the adviser could earn an up front commission on sale and thereafter a small ongoing trail commission for doing nothing further provided that the client remains invested. Commissions are no longer permissible (save in relation to very limited classes of business) therefore this model is no longer effective.

The availability of both up front and trail commissions meant that advisers could earn significant fees for sale of products and would be incentivised to do so on a regular basis once any clawback provisions had expired.

This funding model meant that advisers would often not charge up front fees but instead disclose their commission, which of course was chargeable through product providers therefore the pain of payment by the client was eliminated.

The commercial circumstances – particularly that commissions may be clawed back by the product provider for a period of years – do however mean that advisers must maintain regular contact with clients to maintain trust and continuity of advisory/sales work. If those communications amount to regular fact finding and advice then there can be scope to challenge terms which limit advice to individual product sales.

Ongoing advice – explicit terms

Since the RDR charging terms based on assets under management remain available however the lack of trail commission increases the incentive to work on regular advisory terms and maintain close contact so as to avoid loss of clients.

Ongoing advisory terms can be remunerated by any method (save post-RDR commission is prohibited) agreed between the parties, usually hourly rates or a fee derived from assets under management; performance related bonuses are also seen.

CHAPTER SIX
ISSUES PARTICULAR TO PENSIONS

Pensions often appear as a particular species of portfolio, either on their own or as part of a client's larger portfolio. For many people their most valuable asset, save their home, is their pension fund; and it may be their only vehicle for investments.

Where a client has other invested funds then the pension forms only part of this and the suitability of it must be considered in that context. The simplest balance when looking at an individual with other invested funds could be to apply the same principles across the whole set of pension and non-pension investments.

This is a delicate balancing act between seeking growth within the pension fund contrasted with a desire to preserve the pension fund. As discussed when considering suitability this is a highly fact specific question which necessitates expert advice.

The first consideration when looking at a pension is what the original pension actually is. This is pivotal as final salary (or, in post Pensions Act 2012 parlance, "defined benefit") pensions can be worth significantly in excess of the transfer value they would pay if transferred out. However, they are dependent upon the covenant strength of the fund as they can also run the risk of failure. Therefore, in an advisory context additional rules at COBS 19 are applicable. These require that advice is given (or properly supervised by) a person holding specific additional permissions over and above those required to work as a financial adviser; when considering a dispute such expert advice with the relevant permissions must also be sought.

Stakeholder

Stakeholder pensions are a simple form of pension plan operated by many of the major pension providers within strict statutory controls[1]. In particular fees are limited as these are designed for smaller pension funds and simpler arrangements.

SIPPs

The Self-Invested Personal Pension ("SIPP") is originally a creation of the Finance Act 1989 designed to enable the investor to control their own pension monies and how those monies are invested. As such the SIPP is the logical (although not legal) descendant of the SSAS (an occupational scheme with similarly broad investment controls in the hands of the individual members).

The control over investments allows a broad range of investments to be made subject to HMRC limitations on what the SIPP can hold without tax penalties. As such, residential property is a key exclusion as are other items of clearly personal property. However commercial property is a relatively common investment and, in one example, business owners who also own their business premises can take the rent directly into their pension funds and later sell the property in a tax efficient fashion.

This breadth of scope of investment means that the SIPP can be used as a vehicle for investments which may be sought to be made but otherwise there is no access to funds. A pension fund held within a SIPP can therefore be used to invest across a broad range of investments.

1 Inter alia, the Stakeholder Pension Schemes Regulations 2000 (SI 2000/1403)

The majority of SIPPs are structured as trusts, therefore whilst there is an FCA regulated SIPP operator who undertakes the actions of managing the SIPP there is also a trustee which actually holds the assets of the SIPP. Therefore responsibilities may be shared between more than one legal entity.

The establishment and operation of a SIPP is in itself a regulated activity[2] and requires specific authorisation to do so. However, carrying out other regulated activities which are necessary to effect that work (such as arranging and dealing) does not require additional permissions.

Given the flexibility of the SIPP it is a potential vehicle to effect investments of an unsuitable nature and the FCA has raised concerns[3] regarding the operation of SIPPs and the steps and processes necessary to comply with the regulated duties.

The Lifetime Allowance

Since the imposition of a Lifetime Allowance on the maximum value of a pension fund, there is additional taxation due on funds larger than this. However, for large funds which existed before this was brought in, protection provisions were permitted to exempt such funds from this tax, if such protection was obtained and maintained properly. Hence failures to secure or maintain such protection can give rise to potentially significant claims.

---

2 Article 52, RAO

3 See FCA Finalised Guidance FG 13/08

CHAPTER SEVEN
PRACTICAL ISSUES IN LITIGATION

Protocol

As parties are now required to undertake an appropriate pre-action protocol prior to litigation the choices are between the very generic requirements of the Practice Direction on Pre-Action Conduct or the professional negligence protocol.

This does necessitate significant investigative work to be able to prepare a full letter before action and may involve expert evidence to be able to do so.

A protocol response must be full and the protocol also allows for efforts to resolve the dispute. There is a clear intention that the protocols are designed to narrow the scope of disputes and to avoid criticism, particularly in costs, as to conduct of a case it is necessary to demonstrate reasonable compliance and an intention to narrow, if not resolve, the dispute in pre-action steps.

Expert evidence

As a professional negligence type dispute expert evidence is often needed, subject to the court's permission – which is restricted to that which is necessary to reasonably resolve the dispute.

There is a certain divergence of judicial opinion as to whether expert evidence is necessary and if so directed as to which issues. This does not remove the general principle that to pursue a claim of negligence asserting breach of professional standards will ordinarily require expert evidence as to those standards – and in the financial services context it is important to establish that the expert from whom evidence is sought had appropriate experience at the appropriate time. It can also be necessary to consider other expert evidence, one particular to financial services can be actuarial evidence, to consider, for example, the actual or projected performance of financial instruments.

Proving loss

One of the most important issues to which evidence – particularly of experts – needs to be directed is establishing loss itself. Merely pointing to alternatives is not sufficient and clear evidence as to what would have been done or would have occurred absent the breaches alleged is necessary.

CHAPTER EIGHT
THE FINANCIAL OMBUDSMAN SERVICE

In certain disputes it should be borne in mind that the Financial Ombudsman Service ("FOS") offers a relatively swift means of alternative dispute resolution.

The FOS is considered sufficiently effective that[1] the courts have approved a stay on terms that the dispute be referred to FOS.

FOS is constituted under Part XVI of FSMA and its rules are set out at in the ("DISP") part of the FCA Handbook.

The major differences between FOS and traditional litigation centre around the application of the law, evidential process and costs.

The FOS is not required to apply the law strictly rather s.228(2) FSMA requires:

> *"A complaint is to be determined by reference to what is, in the opinion of the ombudsman, fair and reasonable in all the circumstances of the case."*

This provides scope for fairness in resolving what could otherwise be interpreted strictly.

This is balanced by the lack of disclosure obligations. Therefore where reasonable disclosure may be expected to produce documentary evidence of significant relevance to the case the FOS may

1 Templars Estates v Nat West, QBD (Commercial Court) 10 June 2016, unreported.

request such documents but the parties cannot expect to obtain disclosure. In many cases this may not be problematic as there is sufficient open information available to pursue a complaint properly and direct the FOS to the issues which it can require the other side to address in responding but this cannot be guaranteed.

Whilst there is[2] scope for FOS to make awards of costs this is exceptionally rare. Therefore the costs risk attendant upon litigation are not present.

Time limits at the FOS are slightly different to those in the Limitation Act – instead they are set out in DISP 2.8. Particularly a complaint cannot be brought after 6 years unless within 3 years of date of knowledge. However a complaint is brought for these purposes when received by the firm complained about or the FOS. Once a complaint is received by the firm then it cannot be referred to FOS until either a final response is issued by the firm or 8 weeks have elapsed; however once that final response is issued there is a 6 month period to refer the complaint to FOS. This of course does not affect civil limitation periods.

The effect of FOS decisions can make them very effective for a client. If a decision is accepted by the consumer then it is enforceable as if it were a County Court judgment[3]. If not accepted by the consumer then the decision is of no effect whatsoever – therefore a dissatisfied client can proceed to litigation over the same issue if the FOS does not decide in their favour. Whether such a step is advisable however may depend upon the circumstances of the unfavourable decision and must bear in mind that such a decision may well prove disclosable.

2 s.230 FSMA 2000

3 p.16(a), Part III of Sch 17 of FSMA 2000

Finally, as the FOS does not have a statutory appeal route the options to challenge an unfavourable decision are either to decline the decision and pursue litigation by the complainant against the firm; or (and for an aggrieved firm, the only option) to pursue judicial review of the decision. This should be noted as markedly different to other Ombudsman schemes, such as the Pensions Ombudsman (defined by the Pensions Act 1990, ss.145-152) where there is a statutory right to appeal to the High Court (or another statutorily defined destination of appeal). The case of Westminster v Haywood[4] addressed this issue in detail and made it quite clear that where there is a statutory right of appeal then the Ombudsman could be treated as an inferior court for the purpose of issue estoppel – therefore a failed Pensions Ombudsman case (as in Haywood) would need to exercise that appeal or otherwise the decision would be binding.

4 [1999] EWHC 272 (Ch)

CHAPTER NINE
THE FINANCIAL SERVICES COMPENSATION SCHEME

The final option when facing a firm which has no assets or insurance is to look to the Financial Services Compensation Scheme ("FSCS"). This is a final option as a condition of applying for compensation is that all rights in relation to the subject matter are assigned to the FSCS. Therefore if there are other avenues to redress these may prove more effective.

The FSCS does not however pay compensation automatically in investment type cases. In contrast to banking cases where, once default is established, the FSCS is automatically liable to restore the claimant's position. In investment business cases it is necessary to establish that liability would rest with the firm in default.

The first step in any FSCS claim is to ascertain if the firm in question is actually in default. If not then it is necessary to ascertain if they can be pursued through another avenue instead; or whether an approach must be made to the FSCS to seek to place the firm in default.

The FSCS must investigate the means of the firm, or former firm, and once it is satisfied as to its inability to pay will declare that the firm is in default and the FSCS will meet valid claim against the firm.

Much like the FOS, the FSCS is a creation of FSMA, in this case Part XV, and subject to its own rules set out in the compensation ("COMP") Handbook.

The FSCS scope of claims which it is required to address is set out in COMP 5, particularly COMP 5.2.1 R, specifically of relevance to investment business is COMP 5.5 and the scope of protected investment business.

The FSCS obligation to pay compensation arises in respect of "claims" (being defined in the Handbook glossary) as those civil claims owed by the firm to the client. Once applicable business is found to exist in the context of a firm in default then the crux of the requirements are framed in terms of circumstances where the FSCS must reject (in COMP 8.2) such a claim.

That requirement extends to a bar on the FSCS paying where the claim could have been defeated by a defence of limitation at the time the firm went into default per COMP 8.2.3 R; however this may be disregarded by the FSCS in certain circumstances.

The major practical difficulty with FSCS claims is the absence of a viable defendant from whom to obtain disclosure. This can require significant investigations into the client's means and the circumstances to ensure that a full and clear case is presented. It can also present issues where a firm has wholly failed to comply with the requirement to provide a suitability report and therefore it is necessary to piece together the advice given to establish a prima facie case.

CHAPTER TEN
FUNDING ARRANGEMENTS

One major hurdle in all modern litigation is the cost of undertaking the litigation itself. The two distinct issues are the own costs of solicitors, counsel and experts; and the adverse costs risk of a costs order against a party.

It is not proposed to approach this issue in any depth but merely to highlight areas for further consideration insofar as they relate to financial services claims.

In the first instance, almost all claims are suitable for the multi track due to complexity and depth of evidence – that being they will not be susceptible to resolution in a single day of trial on the fast track. Therefore all the risks and benefits of budgeting post-Harrison[1] apply; so approved/agreed future costs are deemed reasonable and proportionate. This can 'lock in' the costs attributable to each phase (subject only to applications to depart from the budget).

Proportionality is, however, an area upon which there is little clear guidance and a significant breadth of judicial discretion. Therefore for cases where the total of the parties costs significantly exceed the sum in dispute it is necessary to consider carefully the cost/benefit of the case.

When considering budgeting it is also necessary to consider the exposure to adverse costs and whether, in light of the merits of the claim, this is justifiable.

1 Harrison v University Hospitals Coventry & Warwickshire NHS Trust [2017] EWCA Civ 792

There is (at the time of writing) a good market in after the event insurance and where there is a case with merit and value it is absolutely necessary for advice to be given regarding the availability of after the event insurance. Ultimately whether it is taken out is a matter for the client but failing to raise the option is unlikely to be perceived well if the case fails.

It must be noted that damages based agreements under the regulations[2] are permissible in this class of litigation. However the ordinary caution regarding such agreements must be echoed – to comply with the regulations there may be no other provision for the lawyers to be paid under such an agreement.

Notably, litigation funding however has improved dramatically and for cases of significant value this can offer an option to bring cases where other funding may not be available.

Non-litigious case funding

Where a client prefers not to take the litigation option (or opts to do so as a precursor to potential litigation) then it is open to agree a contingency fee agreement. This allows solicitors to agree a fee agreement purely based on the proceeds recovered and, in the context of higher risk cases where the client is commercially aware, such arrangements have received judicial approval in Bolt Burdon v Tariq[3].

However, when contemplating a contingency fee agreement relating to simpler cases there is SRA guidance[4] to be considered.

2 Damages Based Agreements Regulations 2013 (SI 2013/609)

3 [2016] EWHC 811 (QB)

4 http://www.sra.org.uk/PPI

This cautions solicitors to bear in mind the Code of Conduct when acting in such cases, particularly given the simple nature of such cases, when proposing or agreeing such a fee agreement.

CHAPTER ELEVEN
CONCLUSION

The provision of financial services is strictly regulated so as to protect consumers, nevertheless there is scope for mistakes to be made. These can be as simple as overenthusiasm in advising or as complex as systematically poor practice.

The ongoing developments of the legal framework, such as the inclusion of derivatives of emission allowances (or carbon credits) as regulated financial instruments in MiFID II[1], demonstrates this evolution of the regulatory system. Notwithstanding which there continue to be claims arising out of the mistakes made.

It awaits to be seen what new developments 2018 and beyond will bring to this area.

1 EC Directive 2014/65/EU, Schedule C

MORE BOOKS BY LAW BRIEF PUBLISHING

A selection of our other titles available now:

'Arguments and Tactics for Personal Injury and Clinical Negligence Claims' by Dorian Williams
'A Practical Guide to QOCS and Fundamental Dishonesty' by James Bentley
'A Practical Guide to Drone Law' by Rufus Ballaster, Andrew Firman, Eleanor Clot
'Practical Mediation: A Guide for Mediators, Advocates, Advisers, Lawyers, and Students in Civil, Commercial, Business, Property, Workplace, and Employment Cases' by Jonathan Dingle with John Sephton
'Practical Horse Law: A Guide for Owners and Riders' by Brenda Gilligan
'A Comparative Guide to Standard Form Construction and Engineering Contracts' by Jon Close
'A Practical Guide to Compliance for Personal Injury Firms Working With Claims Management Companies' by Paul Bennett
'A Practical Guide to the Landlord and Tenant Act 1954: Commercial Tenancies' by Richard Hayes & David Sawtell
'A Practical Guide to Personal Injury Claims Involving Animals' by Jonathan Hand
'A Practical Guide to Psychiatric Claims in Personal Injury' by Liam Ryan
'Introduction to the Law of Community Care in England and Wales' by Alan Robinson
'A Practical Guide to Dog Law for Owners and Others' by Andrea Pitt
'Ellis and Kevan on Credit Hire – 5th Edition' by Aidan Ellis & Tim Kevan
'RTA Allegations of Fraud in a Post-Jackson Era: The Handbook – 2nd Edition' by Andrew Mckie
'RTA Personal Injury Claims: A Practical Guide Post-Jackson' by Andrew Mckie
'On Experts: CPR35 for Lawyers and Experts' by David Boyle
'An Introduction to Personal Injury Law' by David Boyle
'A Practical Guide to Claims Arising From Accidents Abroad and Travel Claims' by Andrew Mckie & Ian Skeate
'A Practical Guide to Cosmetic Surgery Claims' by Dr Victoria Handley
'A Practical Guide to Chronic Pain Claims' by Pankaj Madan
'A Practical Guide to Claims Arising from Fatal Accidents' by James Patience

‘A Practical Approach to Clinical Negligence Post-Jackson’ by Geoffrey Simpson-Scott
‘A Practical Guide to Personal Injury Trusts’ by Alan Robinson
‘Employers' Liability Claims: A Practical Guide Post-Jackson’ by Andrew Mckie
‘A Practical Guide to Subtle Brain Injury Claims’ by Pankaj Madan
‘The Law of Driverless Cars: An Introduction’ by Alex Glassbrook
‘A Practical Guide to Costs in Personal Injury Cases’ by Matthew Hoe
‘A Practical Guide to Alternative Dispute Resolution in Personal Injury Claims – Getting the Most Out of ADR Post-Jackson’ by Peter Causton, Nichola Evans, James Arrowsmith
‘A Practical Guide to Personal Injuries in Sport’ by Adam Walker & Patricia Leonard
‘The No Nonsense Solicitors’ Practice: A Guide To Running Your Firm’ by Bettina Brueggemann
‘Baby Steps: A Guide to Maternity Leave and Maternity Pay’ by Leah Waller
‘The Queen's Counsel Lawyer's Omnibus: 20 Years of Cartoons from The Times 1993-2013’ by Alex Steuart Williams

www.ingramcontent.com/pod-product-compliance
Lightning Source LLC
LaVergne TN
LVHW022113200926
848481LV00003B/1161